GIFTED
&
TALENTED®

*To develop
your child's gifts
and talents*

LEARN
TO DRAW

For Ages 6 and Up

By Nina Kidd

Lowell House
Juvenile

Los Angeles

CONTEMPORARY BOOKS
Chicago

For my mother

Reviewed and endorsed by Lynn Bennett, M.A., Art Educator at the Curtis School in Los Angeles, and 1993 National Endowment for the Arts Art Education Fellow

Requests for such permissions should be addressed to:
Lowell House Juvenile
2029 Century Park East, Suite 3290
Los Angeles, CA 90067

Lowell House books can be purchased at special discounts when ordered in bulk for premiums and special sales. Contact Department VH at the above address.

Publisher: Jack Artenstein
General Manager: Elizabeth Duell Wood
Director of Publishing Services: Mary D. Aarons
Editorial Director: Brenda Pope-Ostrow
Text Design: Christine Felter Yglesias
Cover Design: Lisa-Theresa Lenthall

Manufactured in the United States of America

ISBN: 1-56565-164-2

10 9 8 7 6 5 4 3 2 1

CONTENTS

Note to Parents 4

How to Use This Book 5

Materials 6

Drawing Tips 7

Starting a Drawing 8

"What Should I Draw?" — Silhouettes 10

A Picture Made With Just Two Shapes 12

The Art of Overlapping 14

The Circle and the Half-Circle 16

The Mystery of the Squares That Aren't Square 18

Crazy Cubes 20

Shadow Magic 22

A Realistic Face 24

Surprising Expressions 26

All Kinds of Faces 28

Facial Features Made of Shadows 30

A Kitten 32

A Dog 34

Copying Animal Shapes 36

Animals From Life 38

Textures 40

A Race Car 42

Close or Far? 44

Scale and Point of View 46

Positive and Negative 48

The Moving Drawing 50

Cups, Caps, Cans, and Cones 52

One-Point Perspective 54

Two-Point Perspective 56

Upside-Down Drawing 58

The One-Line Drawing 60

Blind Drawing 62

GIFTED & TALENTED® LEARN TO DRAW will help develop your child's natural talents and gifts by providing artistic exercises to enhance critical and creative thinking skills. These skills of logic and reasoning teach children **how** to think. They are precisely the skills emphasized by teachers of gifted and talented children.

Thinking skills are the skills needed to be able to learn anything at any time. If a child has a grasp of how to think, school success and even success in life will become more assured. In addition, the child will become self-confident as he or she approaches new tasks with the ability to think them through and discover solutions.

GIFTED & TALENTED® LEARN TO DRAW presents these skills in a unique way, combining the basic subject areas of reading, language arts, math, and visual arts with thinking skills. The top of each page is labeled to indicate the specific thinking and drawing skills developed. Here are some of the skills you will find:

- Deduction — the ability to reach a logical conclusion by interpreting clues

- Understanding Relationships — the ability to recognize how objects and shapes are similar or dissimilar; to classify and categorize, as well as to interpret objects in a different environment (that is, awareness of what is actually seen, such as a three-dimensional object in two dimensions)

- Sequencing — the ability to organize shapes; to recognize as well as create patterns

- Inference — the ability to reach logical conclusions from given or assumed evidence; to extrapolate and work consistently within certain visual conventions

- Creative Thinking — the ability to generate unique ideas; to compare and contrast the same elements in different situations; to imagine the effect of one element upon another in the creation of a visual design; to present imaginative solutions to problems

This book contains drawing exercises that challenge children. The exercises vary in range from easier to more difficult. You may need to work with your child on some of the pages. Each exercise will be labeled as to the level of difficulty, as follows:

 low concentration

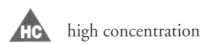 medium concentration

HC high concentration

If necessary, read the directions to your child and explain them. Let your child choose to do the exercises that interest him or her. When interest wanes, stop. An exercise or two at a time may be enough, as the child should have fun while learning. It is important to remember that these drawing exercises are designed to teach your child not only how to draw, but **how to think**.

GIFTED & TALENTED® LEARN TO DRAW has been written and illustrated by a teacher. Educationally sound and endorsed by a leader in the gifted field, this title will benefit any child who demonstrates curiosity, imagination, a sense of fun and wonder about the world, and a desire to learn. This book will open your child's mind to new experiences and help fulfill his or her true artistic potential.

Materials

Here is a list of suggested materials and equipment you will need for the drawing lessons.

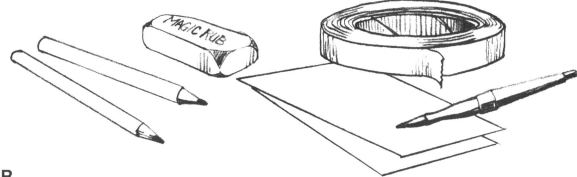

PAPER
9″ x 12″ (or larger) white bond or smooth layout paper,
either a pad or a packet of sheets.

PENCILS
#2 or softer graphite pencils. FaberCastell Design "Ebony" drafting pencils are a good choice. They create a very black line.

ERASERS
Soft pink or white plastic (for example: Eberhard Faber "Magic Rub").
These are for picking out highlights or blending, not just for "mistakes."

DRAWING BOARD
A piece of 14″ x 18″ quarter-inch-thick smooth Masonite is good. You should clip or tape your paper to it. Then you can draw anywhere and at any angle.

TAPE OR BOARD CLIPS
Use drafting-type tape or board clips to attach your paper to the board.
This will avoid tearing.

RULER
Wood with a metal edge is strongest, but any plastic or smooth-edged wood ruler will do.

FIBER MARKING PEN
A black narrow-tip nontoxic marker is good for some of the projects.

OLD MAGAZINES
These will provide pictures of animals, racing cars, or other photos to use as models.

INDEX CARDS Use blank 3″ x 5″ white ones.

COMPASS
You can use one for drawing circles of different sizes. You can also draw the circles by hand.

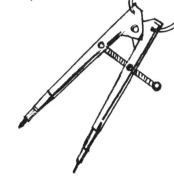

Drawing Tips

There are many different ways to draw, and this book will show you just some of them. Throughout, you will find helpful hints to make your drawings as good as they can be. You can take the skills you learn and go on to create your own special pictures!

HOLDING THE PENCIL For most drawing, you will hold the pencil as you do for writing. However, for some of the exercises (blind drawing, one-line drawing, animals, the racing car, and shadow/faces), hold the pencil **under** your hand (see illustration below). This reminds you to draw by moving your whole arm. Drawing with your whole arm will create a smoother, more even line.

SMEARING If you tend to smear your pencil line with the side of your hand, try putting a clean piece of paper under your hand to protect the drawing. You can remove any smudges with an eraser.

CORRECTING "MISTAKES" If you want to correct a line, don't erase. Instead, redraw right over the original one. It saves time and keeps the drawing looking fresh. If you end up with so many lines that you can't tell which is the right one, start over. Doing your drawing again is good practice. It is better to draw it cleanly and slightly imperfectly than to waste time on corrections.

SAVING A DRAWING When you make a drawing you want to keep, cover it with clean paper until you can frame it or mount it.

Starting a Drawing

Every drawing has edges—a top, bottom, and sides. A picture frame makes a decoration for those edges when you hang it on the wall. But you can draw your own frame, a special decoration that you plan especially for each drawing.

Frames are fun to draw. They can take part of the idea of the drawing and make it into a simple pattern that tells more of the story of the drawing. Here is an example. Now look at the shapes below.

1. Imagine you are making a drawing of a chicken. Imagine you are making a drawing of a fish. Now imagine you are making a drawing of a car. Choose two different kinds of shapes from the ones below that you can combine to make a border design to go with the chicken. Choose two more for a fish border, and two more for a car.

Why did you choose the shapes to go with a particular drawing? Do those shapes remind you of that object or animal?

2. Next, get a piece of paper and a ruler. Then get something rectangular and smaller than your paper, like a book or a magazine. Put the book flat on your paper and draw around it to make a rectangle. Without picking the book up, place the ruler right next to one edge of the book and draw along the outside edge of the ruler. Do the same for each side of the book. When you pick up the book and the ruler, you should have drawn a box with a border the width of the ruler. Erase the extra lines at the corners.

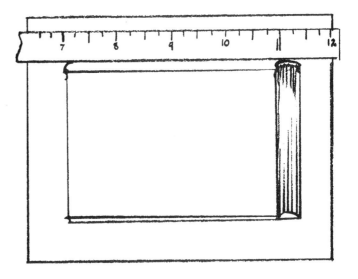

3. Now, pretend you have drawn a chicken, a fish, or a car. In the border outline you have made, try drawing the two shapes you have chosen in a repeated pattern, like 1, 2, 1, 2 or 1, 2, 2, 1, 2, 2, 1. Start from the middle of each side, then go to the corners, repeating the same pattern as the example shows below.

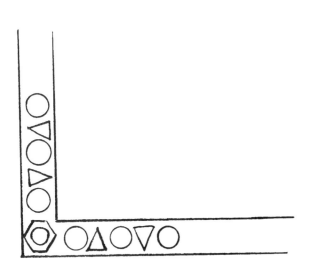

4. A good place to change the design a little is at the corners of the frame. Eyes like to see something bigger or different in each corner. What would still go with your pattern but be a little bit different? Each corner in one border should be the same. Start with something simple: a circle, triangle, or square. How might these shapes fit in your corners? Here's an example of a circle corner pattern. Try to keep your patterns inside the outline you have drawn. Later we'll do some drawing in which your picture breaks right out of the border.

"What should I draw?" — Silhouettes 🄻🄲

Deciding what to draw is one of the hardest parts of getting started. Here is a drawing project that starts with a tracing. What should you trace? How about that object at the end of your arm — your hand? And what about other objects, like the ones in your desk drawer or on your kitchen table?

1. On your paper, draw a broad frame line (see instructions on page 9). This border should be **two** ruler widths instead of just one.

2. Next, trace the outline of your hand and arm as if it's reaching into the picture. Your marking pen is good for this project. Trace the other hand. What could they be trying to reach?

3. Look around your desk and find some things with interesting shapes. The example may give you some ideas. Place the objects on your paper, overlapping either the edge of your frame line, your hand outline, or each other. You may trace the same object more than once.

4. Now you can find new shapes by filling in the traced shapes with patterns — like wavy lines, dots, short groups of lines, arrows, and circles. (You can think of many more!) What happens to the patterns where the shapes overlap? Try coming up with a new pattern for those areas, maybe a combination of the patterns of each one. Add patterns to the shapes **inside** the frame line only.

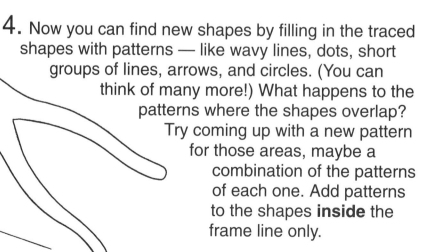

5. Where the traced shapes overlap the broad frame, see if you can make them change again. Should they be solid black? Should they be plain white, with the background of the frame in a pattern or in black? Whatever you choose, try to make it work the same way all around the frame.

6. Now you have created a beautiful design by tracing shapes and using just black and white. Can you say which is the background and which is the object in the frame? If you have trouble deciding, you're right! In a good drawing, the background shapes and patterns are just as important as the main objects.

ON YOUR OWN How could you do this drawing again, tracing the same objects in the same places, but make it look entirely different? (**Hint:** Could the black and white parts of the picture switch places?)

A Picture Made With Just Two Shapes

Here's a challenge. Do a whole drawing using just two simple shapes, the circle and the triangle. To draw the circles, use a compass, or trace smooth-edged bottle caps (like big apple juice jar tops), small jars, or cups. Use a ruler to draw all the triangles.

1. First, use your pencil to draw a circle. How many ways can you make that circle look different? (**Hint:** Would changing its size help?)

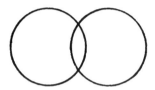 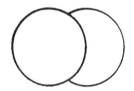 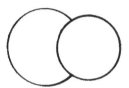

2. Now, how can you combine circles of different sizes to make other shapes? Draw some examples.

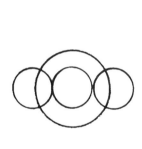 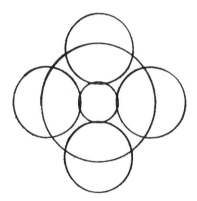 

3. Try combining triangles and circles. Here are just a few examples. Can you think of others?

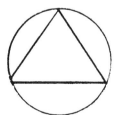 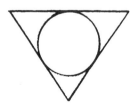 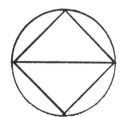

4. Using some of the ideas you have just tried, see if you can draw a whole picture! Draw a border on a large sheet of paper. The example below is the beginning of a picture. The name of your picture will be "A Tree by a River With Mountains in the Background, Using Just Triangles and Circles." Above the picture you can see a few ways to combine the shapes. You will surely find many others. One way to create mountains is to use overlapping triangles. A bush can be made with circles, with a long, skinny triangle shadow. Now try to use these same two shapes to add the tree and the river. Have fun, and don't be afraid to experiment!

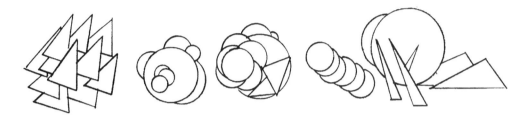

The Art of Overlapping

Overlapping is one way to make some things look closer in a drawing and other things look farther away. In this exercise, see if you can draw shapes and reorganize them to bring some to the front, the back, or the middle. The first drawing on this page shows the combination of shapes drawn just as outlines. In the second drawing, the shapes are like cut-out pieces of paper stacked together. The small circle is on top.

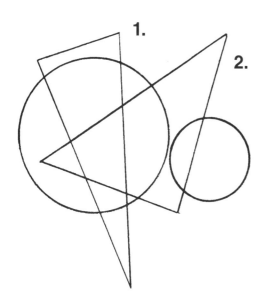

1. First draw the shapes in the same size and same position (trace them if you want to). But draw them so that the triangles look like they are on top of the circles. Triangle #1 (the skinny one) should overlap triangle #2.

2. Draw the same combination again, but this time put the circles on top of the triangles.

3. Now draw the same combination with the small circle on top, triangle #2 next, the big circle next, and triangle #1 on the bottom.

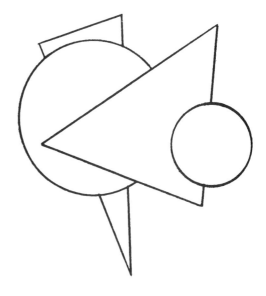

4. Can you make up another arrangement using these same shapes?

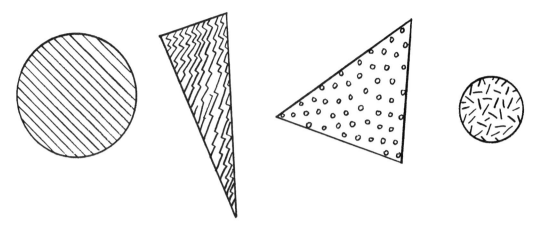

5. Now give each shape its own pattern. The example above is only one way to do it. Below, you can see how different each patterned drawing can be, just by changing the overlapping!

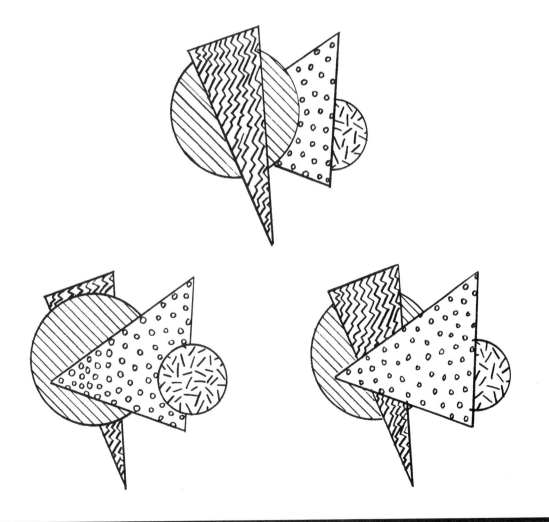

The Circle and the Half-Circle

Here is an exercise in pattern drawing. Use your creativity to see how many ways you can combine two shapes: the circle and the half-circle.

1. In the first exercise, the circles and half-circles should be the same size. (Draw them with the same compass setting or with the same stencil circle.) Can you make five different circular patterns?

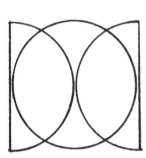 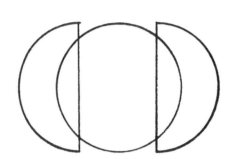 

2. Now the circles and half-circles can be different sizes. You can draw them as if they were cut-out paper. (The shapes can overlap to create new shapes.) Can you come up with ten different border patterns?

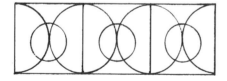 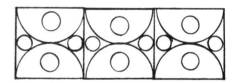

 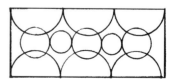

3. Can you create all the shapes below, just by drawing overlapping circles and half-circles? Draw a crescent moon, a two-pointed bead, a sag-sided triangle, a swollen-sided triangle, and a fan.

4. How might you combine circles and half-circles to make a butterfly? A flower? An airplane? (Create your own ideas, different from the examples.)

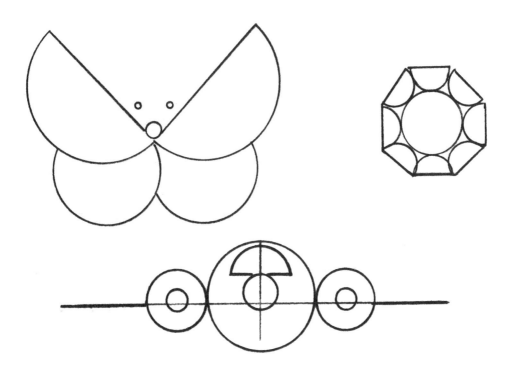

The Mystery of the Squares That Aren't Square

A square has four straight sides all the same length, and four 90-degree angles at the corners. However, while there are many square objects you see every day, if you were to draw them as you **really** see them, your drawings would not contain squares at all! Do you know why? Let's find out.

1. Imagine a card table set up in your living room. The top of the table is a square. If you stand a few feet away and face a **corner** of the table (see the plan at the top of page 19, figure **a.**), what shape is that tabletop to your eyes? Can you draw it?

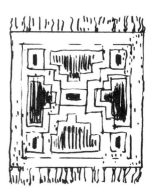

2. Now walk around the table so you are facing one of its **straight sides** (see the plan, figure **b.**). What would you draw to show the tabletop from this position?

3. Next, facing one side of the table again, sit down in a chair (see the plan, figure **c.**). What would you draw for the tabletop? How would it be different from what you drew for figure **b.**?

4. Could you position yourself so that all you see of the square tabletop is just a line? Where would your eyes be in relation to the surface of the table?

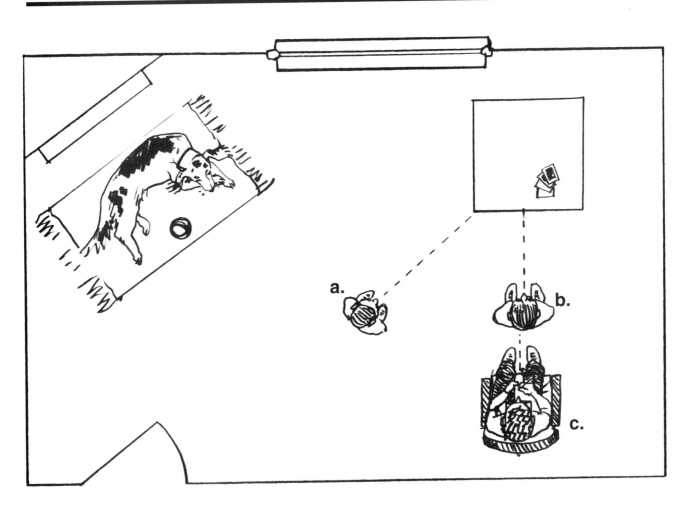

5. **Another Mystery:** You will notice that in your drawings of figures **b.** and **c.**, the edge of the tabletop nearer the bottom of your paper is longer than the tabletop edge nearer the top. That's because even though the edges are really the same length, one edge is closer to you, so it looks bigger. How could you position yourself so that when you draw the tabletop, the top edge of the shape you draw is the longer one? (**Hint:** See the drawing of the girl on page 18.)

ON YOUR OWN   What would happen if the square you are drawing were made of bendy cardboard? How many shapes could you draw just by curving it into an arch? How about bending it so that two diagonal corners curve down toward each other? It would help to cut a 3″ x 5″ index card to 3″ x 3″, then bend it and look at it from different views. You can see that a square is very often **not** a square at all!

Crazy Cubes

Sometimes artists play tricks on us. They draw shapes we are used to seeing on solid objects (such as the crazy cube shown), then put shading or colors on them. The shading makes us think we are not looking at something that sticks **out,** like a solid block, but something that goes **in,** like an open box. How does this work? Do figures **a.** and **b.** on the left look like boxes? Do figures **c.** and **d.** look like little open corners with square roofs? Do the diamonds in figure **e.** look flat? All of these figures are drawn using the same three diamond shapes, in the same size, and in the same arrangement! What is the difference between them?

a.

b.
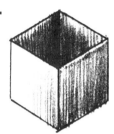

c.

d.
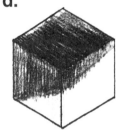

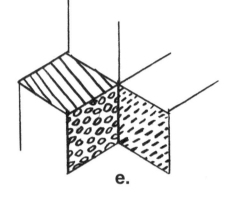
e.

1. Trace the large drawing of diamond shapes to the right. Then see if you can make the shapes look like a stack of cubes, using shading. (**Hint:** Think about which side of a real cube, like a gift box, would be lightest. Which would normally be its darkest side?)

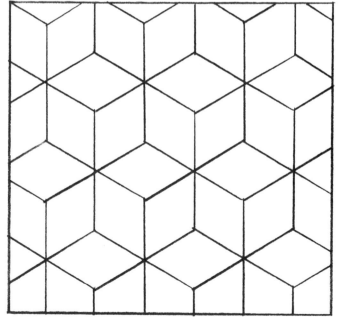

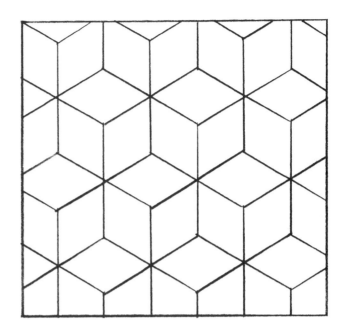

2. Next, trace the same drawing again. See if you can create an all-over pattern on the diamond shapes so that the drawing looks flat (like a pattern on a quilt, for instance).

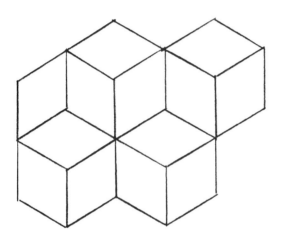

3. Now trace the drawing at the left. See if you can make the three-part hexagons look like open boxes. Feel free to take away a few lines around the edges if they destroy the visual trick you want. You can even add more diamonds to the pattern.

ON YOUR OWN Can you make up any different patterns that fit together and could be made to work the same way as the one in this exercise? Would triangles work?

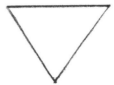

Shadow Magic MC

This is an exercise to help you see the way an artist sees. First, here's a riddle: You are in a flower garden. Your eyes are open, and nothing is covering them. You can smell the flowers, but you can't see them. Why? (See answer below.) One thing that is absolutely necessary for us to see is light. Even if we can't see colors, the contrast between light and shadows allows us to see objects. How does an artist do this? He or she creates pictures of objects using the white of the paper for the lighted areas. The shadow areas, or darks, are made with gentle or heavy pencil marks.

1. How can an artist show a ball bouncing? A cartoonist would use lines to show where the ball landed and what path it is following. But there's another way.

2. Try this: Inside a rectangle, draw a circle for the ball. (**Hint:** Hold the pencil under your hand and draw by moving just your arm. Only the pencil point should touch the paper, not your arm. It may take some practice, but in a short time you will be able to make a nice, smooth circle.)

3. How do you tell a person looking at your picture that it is not a ring, or even a flat circle, but a full, round ball? You can shade it! Usually, light comes from above (the sun, or a light fixture in a room), so the shadow on the ball is on the lower side. As the round surface of the ball turns away from the light, the shadow gradually gets darker and darker. Get a Ping-Pong ball or a baseball for a model. Put it on a piece of white paper under a table lamp. You should shade gradually. When using lines to shade, draw groups of lines that seem to lie on the curving surface of the ball.

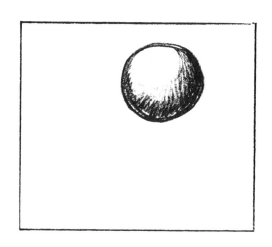

Answer to riddle: It's nighttime!

4. To make your ball look really round, make the darkest part of the shadow just before the lower edge of the circle. Then let the shadow lighten just a bit right next to the edge. This is what you see of the light shining on the surrounding paper as it reflects up onto the dark side of the ball.

5. Now, can you put your ball in motion? How can you show that it's bouncing? Again, use shading. If the ball was on the floor, its shadow would be attached to it. But if the ball was bouncing, the shadow would be separate from the ball. The farther the ball bounces up, the farther it will be from its shadow. (**Hint:** If the shadow is cast on a flat surface, unless you are standing right above it, you must draw the shadow of a ball in the shape of an oval.) Hold your model ball off the paper a few inches and see what happens.

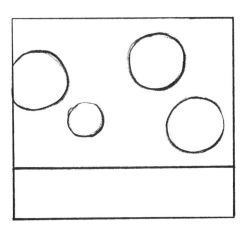

6. What would your ball look like if it was lit by two lights, one on the left and one on the right? (You can use the table lamp and a flashlight to see.) How do its shadows on the table look now?

7. Try drawing a bunch of balls, all bouncing at different heights, in the same picture. Decide if the light is coming from above and to the right, or above and to the left. Then draw the balls and their shadows, so that the light falls on each from the same direction.

A Realistic Face [MC]

When you draw a face, you can make it look quite real if you know a few simple shapes and measurements.

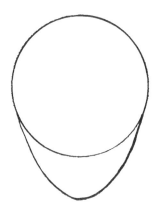

1. Start with the shape of the head and draw a circle. The top part of the human head is shaped like a ball. Now add on below the circle so you have an egg shape, or an oval. The small end of the egg is downward.

2. Divide the egg in half with one light line from top to bottom, then another line crosswise, halfway down from the top. The up-and-down center line is an imaginary midline that runs down through the center of the nose, lips, and chin. The crosswise line halfway down marks where the eyes will go.

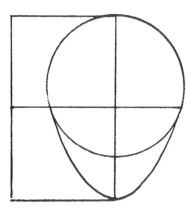

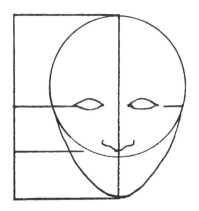

3. Draw the eyes as two almond shapes on the crosswise line, with the big end of the almond toward the center line. There should be a little less than one almond length between them. Draw another crosswise line halfway between the eye-line and the bottom of the egg (the chin). This marks the bottom of the nose. Draw a curvy line about the same length as the space between the eyes, just above this measuring line. This is the bottom edge of the nose.

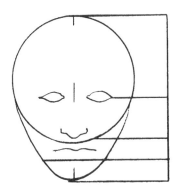

4. The lower lip sits on another imaginary line halfway between the bottom of the nose and the chin. The line of the opening of the mouth is about halfway between the bottom of the nose marker and the lower lip marker. Unless the person is smiling, the corners of the mouth tip down. The corners of the mouth stop directly under the center of each eye.

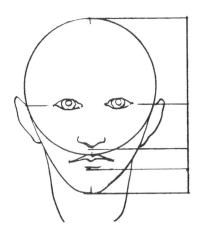

5. From this angle, the ears can look like butterfly wings or narrow banana shapes. However, they almost always attach level with the ends of the eyeline. The ears extend down to level with a point just below the bottom of the nose. The irises (the colored parts of the eyes) are round, and on most people they are partly hidden by the upper and lower lid. The sides of the neck are two lines that bulge slightly and curve inward and down, below the ears, from about the same level as the lip line.

6. Now add the shoulders, which are like a broad triangle with its tip at the chin. The shoulders are just less than two head-lengths wide. Erase all the extra lines, or trace your drawing, leaving out the unneeded lines. Last, add the eyebrows and shapes for the hair. Remember, hair has thickness, like a cloud or a thick layer of frosting on the head. Draw it like a shape first, with shadows on the lower edges that curve in toward the forehead and under at the tips. Notice that the hairline curves in and out around the face. Then you can add the texture: ripply, smooth, wavy, or curly (see page 41 for some ideas about hair textures).

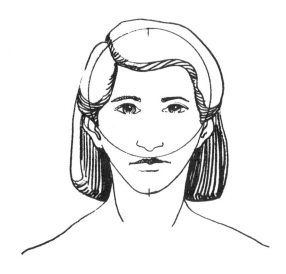

ON YOUR OWN Try drawing a face with rounder eyes, a broader nose, a narrower mouth. On pages 28–29, you will find out how to make a face you draw look silly, or how to make it look like a baby, a man, a woman, or an old person.

Surprising Expressions

Do you know which three features on the human face do the most to express what the person is feeling? Of course, the mouth is one. You know that a mouth widens to make a smile, but the eyes and the eyebrows are just as important.

1. Eyebrows can go up, down, be joined together, or twist (part up and part down). Look in a mirror and pretend for a moment that you are surprised. Which way do your eyebrows go? Now pretend that you're mad! What if you were suspicious?

See how your eyebrows work for different expressions, like fear, surprise, anger, or sadness. Here are some examples. Can you think of a name for each expression?

2. Eyes change shape and open and close to show emotion, too. Which are the sad eyes? Which are happy? Angry? Can you name an emotion for each pair of eyes?

3. Mouths can be tiny, big and round, or twisted up at one corner, down at the other. Again, pick the feelings that go with these mouths.

4. Now you can trace the faces below, or copy the outlines and make your own expressions. What would happen if you mix up "fear" eyebrows with "surprise" eyes?

ON YOUR OWN You can make many blendings of feelings by trying different combinations. Hair can even add to the expression. Have you ever heard of people being so scared, their hair stands on end? Can you imagine what "sad" hair looks like? What about "happy" hair?

All Kinds of Faces MC

There are some basic rules for drawing a human face, but there are many kinds of faces to draw. How can you make a person look like a baby? How about an old woman? Below, you can see a young adult male in the middle picture. His face follows the basic proportion rules. Notice that the proportions are different for the child. Try to draw all the faces on this page, starting with the basic face shape you learned on pages 24 and 25.

1. A baby has a big head in relation to its body, large eyes, and a small lower face in relation to the rest of its head. Draw in this baby's eyeline, just below halfway from the top of his head to his chin. He also has a small chin. This is partly because he doesn't have his grown-up teeth yet. They will make the face longer. His cheeks are rounded and his chin is pointed.

2. As a person passes middle age, the muscles aren't as tight, the thin layer of fat under the skin goes away, and the skin begins to sag. Notice how the old woman's eyes tilt down. Her cheeks hang down and make creases on either side of her nose. Her nose and ears can get longer, and her chin gets squarer. Of course, you can add wrinkles, too.

3. Try looking around at the people you know to see different kinds of features. Here are just a few kinds of eyes. They can be slanted, tilted up or down, wide or narrow, large or small, bulgy or deep set.

4. Noses, too, can be many shapes — rounded, fat, thin, long, bumpy, flat, turned up, turned down, or even twisted over to one side. The first row contains children's noses. They are usually smaller and more rounded than grown-ups' noses. The second row contains grown-ups' noses.

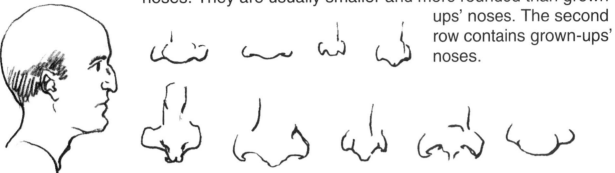

5. How do you make a man's face look like a man, and a woman look like a woman? Hairstyles can help, but there are some basic differences. The center face below is neither male nor female. Notice that the man has a more bony face. His chin is squarer. His lips are usually not as rounded and full, and his eyebrows are straighter and heavier. A woman has more rounded, thinner eyebrows. Her cheeks tend to be smoothly rounded, and her chin is more pointed. Women's necks are usually more slender, and their noses are usually smaller than men's, too.

ON YOUR OWN Have some fun making characters by moving features around. The head shape could be upside down; the eyes too high, too far apart, or close together; the face long and thin or wide and fat. Try to draw lots of faces using different features. Some of them can be silly!

Facial Features Made of Shadows MC

If you have been drawing for some time, you have probably learned some ways to draw faces. The eyes can be egg shapes with eyelashes, and the nose can be a pickle, a triangle, or a ball. The mouth can be a line or a heart. How can you make your faces look more real? Try forgetting what you know about eyes, the lashes, the irises, and begin to think about the face as if it were a stone sculpture — all one color, with light falling on it. Now you can make a very real-looking face by just filling in its shadows.

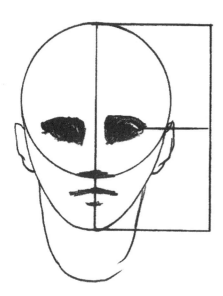

1. Start with the face shape you learned on pages 24 and 25. Put the halfway line in where the eyes will be. Think of the eyes as balls that are set into squarish holes in a person's head. If you see a person in the bright sunlight, sometimes you don't see his or her eyelids, pupils, or lashes at all. What you see is a squarish shaded area — the whole eye socket. Look for a photograph or a picture in a magazine of a face in bright light. Try copying the shape of the whole eye-socket area. Use only shading, no outlines.

Here are two examples drawn from a photo. You can see the eyelids and eye-brows, but the whole eye area is dark.

girl

boy

2. A nose is basically a three-sided triangle that sticks out from the face and slopes gradually to the cheeks on either side. Again, when you look at a nose in the light, you don't see its edges on either side, so don't draw them. Draw only the shadow it makes: the shadow of the nose on its own underside, and on the lip below.

3. The mouth, if you create it out of shadows, is the shape of the upper lip, which usually is turned away from the light, creating a shadow shape. There should be a shadow under the lower lip, too. The lower lip itself is in the light, like the nose, but don't draw the outline of the darker lip color. Remember, you are pretending this is a stone face — all one color. The only **line** you should draw for the mouth is the line where the lips come together. Unless the person is smiling, the lip line goes down a bit at its outer corners, up toward the middle, with a bit of a dip in the very center. Look at yourself in the mirror to see this.

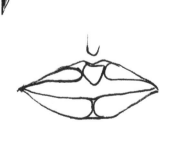

A Kitten MC

You can use the simple shapes of a triangle, a kidney bean, an oval, part of a circle, and a rectangle to draw an animal. Let's try a kitten.

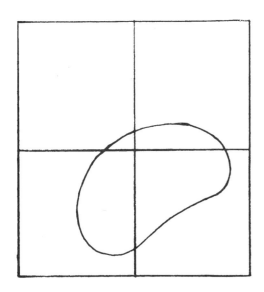

1. Draw an outline on your paper. Inside the outline, begin with a kidney bean. Make the bean the same size as in the example, and in the same place in the outline as the example shows. (The crosswise and up-and-down lines are there just to show you where to draw the bean.)

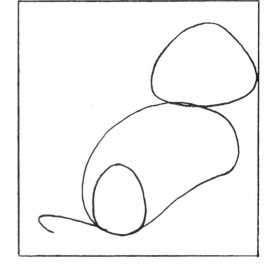

2. Add a rounded triangle for the head, an oval for the hindquarter, and a hooked line for the lower edge of the tail.

3. Add a small circle for the cat's muzzle, parts of circles for the ears, ovals for the forelegs and the hind foot, and then add the upper edge of the tail.

4. Now add football shapes for the eyes, a triangle for the nose, and ovals for the forefeet.

5. Draw in the oval pupils of the eyes, the mouth and chin, and the divisions for the toes. Then erase any unnecessary lines and smooth the joins between the legs and feet and the ears and head.

6. Finally, add the texture of the fur, making sure the fur lines follow the shape of the body. You can make this a tiger kitten by drawing the stripes. The stripes curve around the animal's body, tail, and legs. They are darker on the top and fade as they reach toward the belly.

A Dog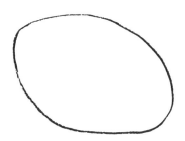

Here's another animal you can practice—a dog. You'll recognize some of the same shapes you used for the kitten on pages 32 and 33. The dog is a bit more complicated. If you need to, you can trace a rectangle around the fourth drawing (top of page 35). Then draw the same-size rectangle on your paper. You can use the sides of the rectangle to get the correct sizes of each shape, and to tell where each new shape should be drawn.

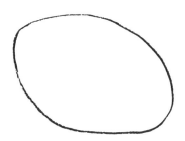

1. Start with a football shape, slightly flattened on the bottom, for the chest.

2. Now add an egg, small end down, overlapping the chest shape, for the hindquarters. Then add ovals for the upper forelegs, and a chubby triangle for the neck.

3. Draw in an oval for the upper part of the head and ovals for the feet. Draw in the upcurved tail.

4. Add another egg shape for the muzzle, triangles for the ears, part of an oval for the left hind leg, and connecting lines for the legs.

5. Next draw lines for the toes, a leaf shape for the eye, a triangle for the nose, then add the curved mouth opening and tongue. Add the eyebrow ridge over the left eye, and the inside edges of the ears. Erase all the unneeded lines.

6. This is a shaggy terrier-type dog. Fill in the eyes and nose, then draw shorter and longer curving lines for the fur. It is short and smooth on the back and feet, and it gets longer on the face, the lower part of the body, and the backs of the legs. Try to leave a little white dot in the eye for a highlight. It will help the dog look perky!

Copying Animal Shapes MC

You might want to copy an animal from a photograph or a picture in a book. Here are two very different creatures, a Tyrannosaurus and a hummingbird. Try following the directions below, and you may be surprised at how accurately you can copy the drawings. Notice that the dinosaur has been put in a square. In the earlier steps of the Tyrannosaurus, the box has been divided into four sections. This gives you edges so you know if the shapes you are drawing are copied correctly. First draw the same square on your paper (it can be much larger than the example, but the proportions must be the same). Then divide it in half, up and down and side to side, so you have four boxes.

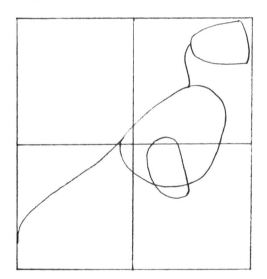

1. Start the Tyrannosaurus in its square by drawing a big flattened pear shape for the body. Then draw a long line from the top of the head to the tip of the tail. The head, with its open mouth, fits inside a round-cornered triangle, and the upper leg is a long oval.

2. Add a fat oval for the foreleg area and long ovals for the lower legs.

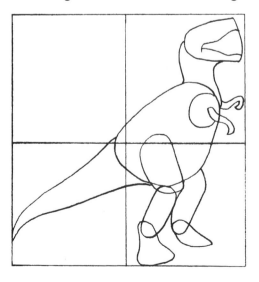

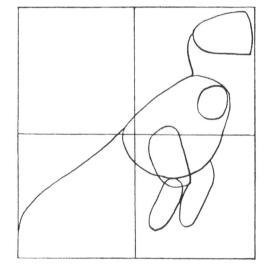

3. Now draw the paddle-shaped feet and thin forelegs. Make a curvy opening for the jaws. Add the lower edge of the thick tail. Notice where it attaches to the pear-shaped body.

4. Next you can add the bumps over the eyes, the small eye, the nostril, and guidelines for the teeth. Draw in the toes and thick toenails. Make a line from just under the foreleg to mark the division between the underside of the body and tail and the upper skin. Now erase any unneeded lines, and smooth out the lines that connect the body parts.

5. Last, add some shading by making the lines curve around the body to show its shape. After you add individual teeth, all the same size, you have a very fierce Tyrannosaurus!

ON YOUR OWN Try drawing the hummingbird the same way. Draw in the background rectangle, then start with the biggest shapes of the body and wings. Then add the smallest shapes of the nostril, the eye, and the feathers. Add feather texture to the wings like very fine overlapping fans. Later, find another animal in a book or a magazine. Draw a rectangle around it, then a matching rectangle on your paper, and see how well your new skill works!

Animals From Life

If you have a pet — a bird, a cat, or a dog — it can be a model for your drawings. Even if you don't have a pet, you can find a photograph of an animal in a magazine and use it as a drawing model.

1. Prepare a piece of drawing paper by making a border with your ruler. Clip the paper to a stiff drawing board. Plan to draw your pet while it's resting, so it will be still. Then position yourself so you can see the pet's face and as much of its body as possible. (Don't try to draw just your dog's head and paws sticking out of the doghouse, for instance.)

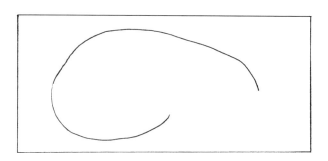

2. Look at the animal. Can you find one long line that you will build the drawing on? It will probably be a line along the neck, back, and tail. Draw this long line, leaving plenty of room to add the animal's head, legs, and feet.

3. Now find the biggest shape of the animal's body. Forget about the shape as you know it to be, or the way you've drawn it before. Draw what you see. The body can be an oval, a kidney bean shape, or even a fat triangle. Add this body shape on the long line, still leaving room for the legs, neck, and head.

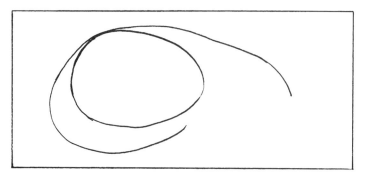

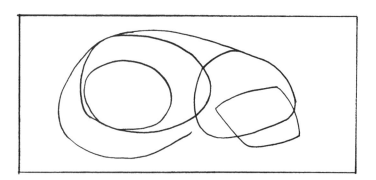

4. What are the next smaller shapes? They are probably the hindquarters, the shoulders, and the upper forelegs. Draw these, making sure they are placed correctly on your first long body line. Look at these big shapes. Compare them with the animal. Are they the right sizes and tilted in the proper directions?

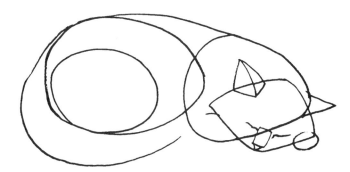

5. Draw in the head as one shape. Is it a triangle? A diamond? A circle with a flat side? Compare the size of the head shape with the hindquarters and adjust them to match the model. Then draw the eyes, ears, and nose.

6. Next complete the tail and add the toes. You have done a rough sketch which should have taken about five minutes. Now erase any unneeded lines.

7. After you have erased the construction lines, thicken the lines where the animal touches the floor or whatever it is lying on. This gives it weight and shows that it casts a shadow.

8. Finally, draw in the texture of its fur. Start with the lower side. Leave the upper side plain, because this is where the light is the strongest. Make the texture lines in each area all go in the same direction. They should wrap around the animal's body.

Textures

With your pencil, you can draw an amazing variety of surfaces: fur or hair, feathers, wood grain, pebbles, or even made-up textures.

1. Fur is made up of lots of lines, usually short ones, slightly curving and all running somewhat in the same direction. If the fur is on an animal, like this tiger's face, the drawn fur texture can curve to show that it is lying on a rounded shape, not just on flat paper. Practice making short, light fur lines with your pencil. Notice that the start of each line is thicker, and that where you pick the pencil up is tapered and thinner. This is perfect for fur. The thick blunt end is near the skin, and the thin, tapering end is at the tips. When you draw an animal, turn your picture as you draw in the fur so all your pencil strokes go in the direction of real fur.

2. The lines in wood grain seem to flow like water around the place where a branch was attached (the knot). This is a good texture for practicing shading from nearly white with lots of grays, to darker and darker, to black. Try to make your lines go from thicker to thinner by pressing hard, and then gradually more gently, as you draw the line.

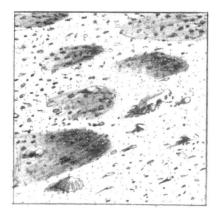

3. What can your pencil do besides draw lines? How about dots? With patience, you can make a texture of sand, with dots darker and closer together in places where you have shadows on the sand. Add a few larger roundish shapes for tiny pebbles.

4. Now put your pencil on its side for a very special effect. If your paper is thin (like newsprint or typing paper), you can make the surface below show up by rubbing the side of your lead gently and evenly over it. Try different surfaces: unfinished wood, a kitchen grater, a window screen, fanned index cards, or even a coin. Can you think of other surfaces?

5. Now try hair. Use long lines, many following nearly the same path, and also following the roundness of the person's head. Whether smooth or very curly, look for the large shapes hair makes. Its tip ends are finer and tend to cling together. Make it gradually darker and lighter to create a shiny effect.

6. Try combining lines and smooth shading made by the side of your pencil to draw a leaf. First pick a leaf with a strong vein pattern to copy. Lightly draw in its veins. Now gently shade the leaf where it curls away from the light. You can make the shading very smooth by rubbing the pencil with a little pad made of facial tissue. Do you want to make a highlight on the leaf? You can easily erase a white highlight with the edge of a soft pink or white eraser.

ON YOUR OWN How many other textures can you make? How about shiny chrome bicycle handlebars, or the bumper of a car? How about water, or clouds? Try to draw as many textures as you can.

A Race Car   MC

Cars don't have to be hard to draw. You can copy pictures from magazines, look at real cars, or design your own if you know what shapes to use. Let's make a race car, designed like the Indianapolis 500 cars.

1. Start with the body of the car, which should be a long and slim rectangle. The front, or nose (right end), should be extended in a triangular shape. This will make the car more aerodynamic, so air can move over it more quickly and it can go faster. The rear, or tail, should be broken up by a shorter triangle.

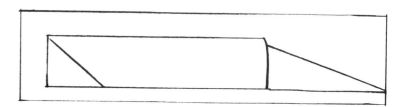

2. Next draw the tires. Basically they are drawn as circles, with the top of a second circle showing behind the first so you can see the tread surface and know how broad the tires are. Smaller circles inside the larger ones show where the rubber tire meets the metal wheel. The front tires are smaller and closer together than the rear ones, so draw the front circles smaller and slightly higher on your picture. Draw in the side of the car as a rough bullet shape. Next draw the shallow cut-out for the cockpit and shapes for the driver's helmet and the roll bar. Add another line from the end of the bullet shape to the extreme front of the car to show the near edge of the wedge-shaped nose.

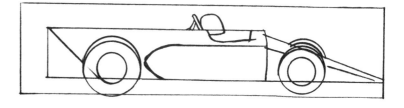

3. Draw the wing shapes, which are the side supports for the spoiler, up behind the tail. The spoiler is the fin that keeps the rear wheels down hard on the track at high speeds. From this angle, all you can see is the side.

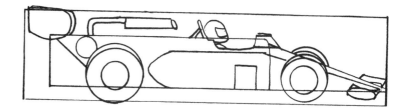

4. Add the circular gas tank behind the rear wheel, then the air intake pipe that runs parallel to the top of the car body and comes down by the tank. Add the wedge for the windshield and the square, which is a hole on the side. Next draw the front spoiler, which keeps the front wheels down. It has two long ovals, with straight edges that run from the ends of the near oval to the far one. Don't forget to add the driver's shoulder!

5. It's fun to make a car look like it's actually racing. You can do this by squeezing it out longer than it really is and changing your tires from round to more oval. It will look as if every part of your car has been pushed down on the road from behind and

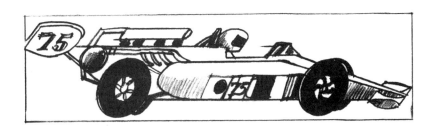

has partly collapsed. You can add the branching pipe of the manifold, which is part of the engine, above the rear tire. Also add shading to the sides of the car, the tires, the spoke holes in the wheels, and the helmet visor. Then add racing numbers.

6. Finally, add the shadow of the car on the ground. Then add speed lines off the tops of the spoiler, the tires, the wheel covers, and the windshield to really make the car look like it is speeding. Draw these lines quickly with a ruler, starting on the car. As you lift your pencil up at the left, the lines should get thinner and seem to fade away toward the rear of the car. Last of all, add dust!

Close or Far? MC

When you look at a picture, you can imagine even the simplest shapes are closer to you or farther away by how they look compared to one another. Things that are farther away are _____ (**bigger** or **smaller**?) than things that are close. Also, things that are farther away on the ground look either _____ (**higher** or **lower**?) in a picture than things that are near. How about objects in the sky?

1. Try drawing a scene with trees, bushes, cows, or cars that are all the same. But make some smaller and higher in the picture to make the picture look as if you are looking out a window into real space.

2. What would happen if you broke the rules and put the smaller objects lower on the page and the bigger ones higher? Do the objects look nearer and farther away, or does the picture look flat?

3. It helps to make the space look real if you draw in a pathway into the background. Here is a road across country. Everything gets smaller as it goes away from you and closer to the horizon. The clouds and the bushes are smaller. The road gets narrower, and its curves get closer together.

4. Now let's add some shadows, so that someone looking at the picture can tell that it is a real scene. In this picture, be sure all the shadows run down the right side of each cactus and onto the ground to the right of it. Be sure that each object has its shadow, even the small rocks. The darkest shadows are on the nearest objects. See how the shadows on the hills in the background are only light gray? You can see that this is true when you go outside. Compare the darkness of the shadows of nearby objects and more distant ones.

5. Here are some California palm trees to help you practice your darker to lighter shadows. Welcome to Hollywood!

Scale and Point of View

Here are a number of objects drawn from different perspectives, or points of view. How can you tell whether they were seen from the perspective of an ant, a giant, or a person of average height? Is each object large or small? (**Hint:** It has nothing to do with the size of the drawing. Does it depend on where the object is in relation to the edges of the picture, or something else? You decide.)

1. Could the drawing on the right be a lighthouse? If you add windows and light rays, it could be. Actually, it is a salt shaker, seen from the level of the table. How could you tell? One way would be to add details to the object that tell you exactly what it is. Maybe you could draw this picture so it is both a salt shaker **and** a lighthouse. The doorway is a start.

2. What about this rectangular solid? The trees tell you it must be a building. But what else could it be? Try tracing it and replacing the palm trees with something that tells you this object is small enough to pick up in your hands. What familiar object would tell you for sure that this is not a building?

3. Is there any way you know this is a ball? You can't change your point of view so the ball looks different. Balls are the same from all sides! Scale is a good way. What could you put in the picture to show the ball is the size of a pea? How about the size of a balloon?

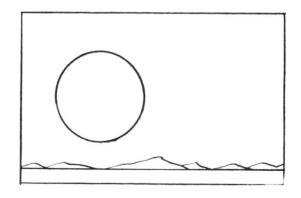

4. Compare the two drawings below. Where are you as you look at the first man? Where are you as you look at the second man? Does the first one look like a giant? He isn't any bigger than the second man. The artist can tell you this is a giant by looking up from below and changing your point of view.

5. You can make unusual drawings using new points of view. How about a cat from the point of view of a mouse? Can you see now why mice run away?

ON YOUR OWN   Try drawing some other unusual points of view. How about your house as an airplane pilot might see it as he or she comes in for a landing? What about your breakfast table as seen by an ant standing next to your spoon? Use your imagination!

Positive and Negative MC

Certainly you can tell the difference between the subject of a drawing and its background. Or can you?

1. Look at the first drawing. Is it a white candlestick, or two people in darkness facing each other? **Answer:** Either one is correct. The subject is near the viewer and the background is farther away. If you had a choice of using just black and white in a drawing, which would you choose for a background, black or white? If you said black, you are right. Dark areas seem to be farther away from your eye, while white areas usually seem closer. But not always!

2. Could the second picture be blocks with holes between them? You could choose either the black squares or the white ones to be the blocks. Suppose you draw a scene in the white spaces as if you are looking at bits of it between the black squares. Now which is the background?

3. Usually we think of the background as the larger area that touches the corners of the picture. Can you see that this is a picture of two white arrows, one up and one down? The small black shapes are the background. See if you can design a puzzle like this and try it out on a friend.

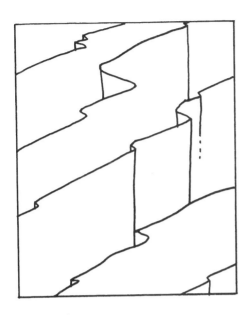

4. Is this a picture of ribbons, or something else? Try tracing it and taking away some of the up-and-down lines to make it look like a flat-topped area with jagged cracks.

5. Artists make use of black and white quite often. The two drawings below are the same; just the colors have been changed. Which curvy "X" shape looks larger, the black or the white one?

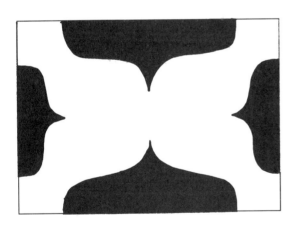

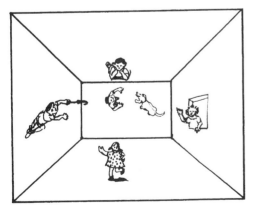

6. How many ways can you see this space? Can it be a room, as shown by the girl in the spotted dress? Can it be a room that we are looking down at from the ceiling? Can the square in the center be sticking out at you? The drawing tells you many different things about this space. If you think it's fun, try drawing a puzzle picture of your own.

The Moving Drawing MC

Here's a fun project — a cartoon you can draw and put into motion yourself. You will need twenty small sheets of stiff paper (blank 3″ x 5″ cards are good).

1. In the lower left-hand corner of each card, make a simple drawing of something that moves (a face that can change expression, or a stick figure of a person or an animal). The example shows how you could make a moving drawing of a face. Plan the entire "story," so you know what your subject should be doing and how much it should change on each card.

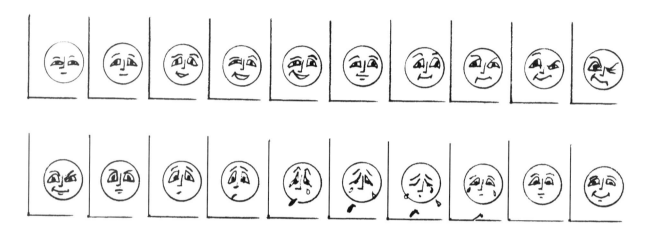

2. On the tenth card, your subject should be halfway through the action like the example, which shows a wink. By the twentieth card, the face has finished winking, it has lost and found a mouth, and it is in the midst of a smile. In between, you will draw the subject changing slightly on each card. To make this cartoon work, the circle for the face must stay in the same place on each card, and only the features must move.

3. When you are finished, put the cards in order and bend them down with your thumb and snap them up, or let go of them, one by one. The face will come alive! This is the way TV or motion picture cartoons are made. In the best movie cartoons, you see twenty-four different drawings on the screen every second!

4. You can either copy the faces shown, or make up a picture of your own. To make the action look real, use a model. Look at yourself in the mirror and imagine how you would crouch down to start a back flip, or just smile and wink (if you are just going to draw your face). You can even look at a dog chasing a ball. (See the examples below.)

ON YOUR OWN Try another cartoon (of a rocket taking off, an animal jumping, or even a person running). The more carefully you observe how these things really look as they move, the more lifelike your handmade cartoons will be.

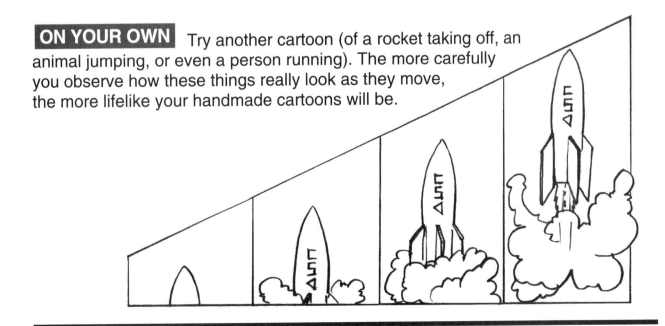

Cups, Caps, Cans, and Cones

Some of the shapes you see most often are based on the circle: the cylinder, the cone, and the half-sphere (or half-ball). If you know how to draw these, you will have no trouble drawing a vase, a soup can, a round building, a column for a building, a tree trunk, a drinking straw, or part of a hat. A cone might be the basis of an ice-cream cone, a fir tree, a sprig of flowers, a bunch of grapes, a chandelier, or a clown's hat. A half-sphere might become a flower, a coffee cup, a lampshade, a hat, foliage on a tree, or an umbrella.

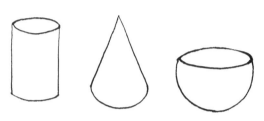

1. All of these shapes are based on the circle, but when the circle is part of an object, as it turns one way and another, it changes shape. Draw a circle. Imagine that your circle is a ring. From the edge it is a line. Spinning on its edge it becomes an oval. It is a wide oval if you're looking nearly through the center. It is a narrow oval as one edge gets nearer to you and the other turns away.

2. Now draw the circle as the top and bottom of a cylinder, like a soup can with its ends cut out. You can see one circle inside the other. Usually, though, you see the cylinder at an angle. The sides are straight lines and the top is a long oval. The bottom is another oval. However, if the can is solid sided, you can see only the lower edge of that oval. Unless you are very close, or the cylinder is as large as a building, the two ovals are about the same size and width.

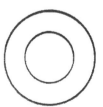  

3. Try drawing a soup can on a low table so that the end of the can looks nearly round to you. Try putting it on the desk or table where you are sitting, then on a high shelf so you can't see the top of it. If you

 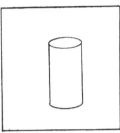 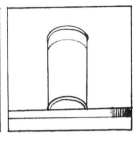

were to draw stripes at the top and bottom of a piece of paper and paste it on the can, like a label, you could see that the stripes follow the curving edges of the bottom and top of the can.

4. Now try a teacup. It has an oval top edge, and the lower half of a ball or sphere for the part that holds the liquid. Add a base with a curving lower edge so the cup won't tip over.

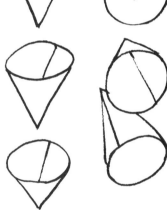

5. Next try a cone, which, when you draw it, also has an oval top edge. As the oval gets wider and you see more of the inside of the cone, the triangle gets shorter. Use a cone to draw a fir tree. The tips of each row of branches touch an oval, and the ovals near the top of the tree get smaller and smaller.

ON YOUR OWN How many of these other shapes can you find in your own house? Draw as many as you can.

One-Point Perspective

In a one-point perspective drawing, you can make a flat piece of paper look like a doorway (or a window) with space for a long hall beyond. This happens because all the going-into-space lines come together at one point, called the vanishing point.

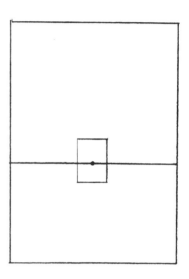

1. Using your ruler, draw a border inside the edges of your paper. Just below the middle of the page, inside the border, lightly draw a level crosswise line. This will be the horizon or eyeline. Put a dot on the eyeline in the center. The dot, or vanishing point, represents the spot directly above where you stand as you face the picture. Now draw a small rectangle around the dot. This will be the open door at the far end of the corridor.

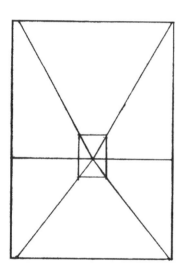

2. Starting from the dot, draw four diagonal lines with your ruler, each one running directly through the corners of the rectangle and out until it stops at the border. (The lines don't have to run right through the corners of your frame.)

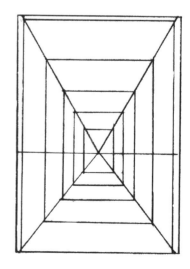

3. Now draw a second box around the first box, its corners on the diagonal lines from the center dot, and its sides a bit thicker than the first. Then draw a third box, also on the diagonal lines and a bit bigger, even farther from the second box than the second is from the first box. Finally, draw a fourth box farther yet from the third box.

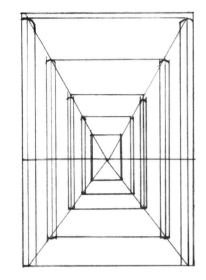

4. The sides of each one of these boxes will become columns. The biggest box respresents columns closest to you, so they should be thickest. Each pair of columns, as you go toward the center, is farther away, so each one should get thinner. Draw them like cylinders, with rounded tops and bases.

5. You can make a fancy arched roof using half-circles. Draw the tops of the columns like upside-down skirts. Then, using your compass, put the point of the compass on the center of the top of each box, extend it sideways to just inside the edge of the skirts, and draw a half-circle. Then change the size on the compass to draw a double half-circle on each box. You can draw the half-circles neatly by hand, too. Then erase the top and bottom lines of the boxes.

6. To make the columns and arches look solid, shadow one side of them as if the sun were shining on them from the right. Draw shadows with side-to-side lines at the base of the columns, so they look like they are resting on a floor.

7. If you want to draw mysterious robed figures in the hallway, make them like round-topped tall triangles and give them shadows, too. (**Hint:** The figures get smaller in the same way that the columns become shorter when they are closer to the eyeline dot.)

Two-Point Perspective

The hallway with columns on page 55 is drawn with one-point perspective. A second kind of in-space drawing uses two-point perspective. It's great for drawing boxlike objects such as books, furniture, train cars, and buildings. In this kind of picture there are two vanishing points on the eyeline, or horizon.

1. Let's draw a box first. With your ruler, draw a frame that is 8″ high by 10″ wide. Draw a line across the rectangle a little above halfway from the bottom. This is your horizon, or eyeline. Make two dots on the eyeline as the example shows. Between the dots and below the eyeline, draw a straight-up-and-down line. (**Hint:** Make sure the line is off center, slightly closer to the left edge of the frame than the right edge.) This is the closest corner of your box.

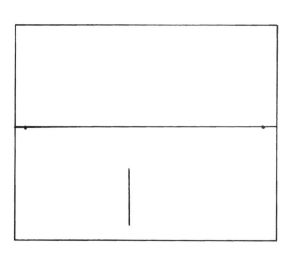

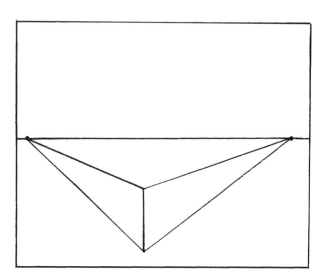

2. Now draw straight lines to the two points on the eyeline. Draw one from the top of the straight-up-and-down line to the dot on the right. Then draw one from the top of the straight-up-and-down line to the left dot. Next draw two more lines from the bottom of the straight-up-and-down line to the right and left dots on the eyeline. You have drawn two triangles. These are the top and bottom edges of the sides of the box closest to you.

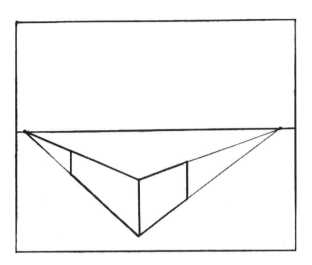

3. Decide how wide and long you want the box to be. Draw an up-and-down line on the left triangle to be the end of the box. Then draw another up-and-down line on the right triangle to show where that side ends. You now have the sides of the box outlined.

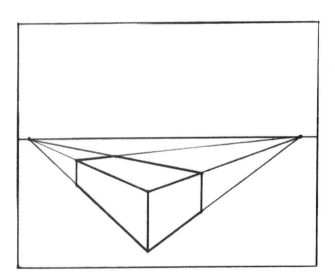

4. To finish the top of the box, draw two more lines. Draw one from the dot on the eyeline near the right edge of your drawing to the top left edge of your box. Draw another from the eyeline dot on the left to the top right edge of your box. Erase the unneeded lines beyond the edges of the box. Your box is now complete!

ON YOUR OWN Try making tall, narrow boxes, or short, flat boxes. The boxes can look different if you move the points on the eyeline closer together and change the height of the near corner of the box. Try drawing a building. Make the first near-corner line extend higher than the eyeline, or horizon. You usually don't see the tops of buildings, so you would just see two sides. Try including windows and/or doors like the picture.

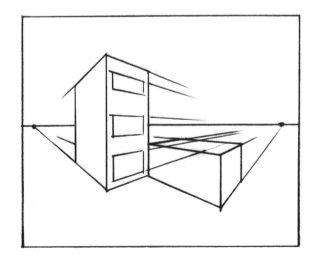

Upside-Down Drawing

This is a drawing made of simple lines, but it is a realistic drawing of a boy and his toy horse. (Turn the book around so you can see the drawing on page 59 the right way, then turn it back.) You can learn to copy this upside-down drawing surprisingly easily by following these directions.

1. Start with a piece of scratch paper and copy the triangle, the circle, and the square, leaving plenty of space between them. Now draw rectangles, and redraw the three shapes in the same places in the rectangles as the examples show. Are they the same? Use your eyes to measure how far they are from the edges of the rectangles and compare them to the examples. This is an exercise to help you draw the large picture later. If you didn't draw the shapes in quite the right spots, try again until you are happy.

2. Now, on a large piece of paper, use your ruler to draw a rectangle that is 8½″ wide by 11″ tall. Next, divide your 8½″ by 11″ box into four equal smaller rectangles (make the lines light), each one 4″ wide by 5½″ tall. Using tracing paper, measure and draw dividing lines over the example on page 59, too.

3. Now look at the example as it is — upside down. On your paper, start at the lower left-hand corner box. Copy the lines you see in the lower left-hand section of the drawing. As you work, both your drawing and the example in the book should remain upside down. Work in the lower left section of the drawing until it's complete. Then go on to the section above it.

4. If you are about halfway done and you don't know which part you are drawing, but you are just working on the shape, you're doing it right! Copy the drawing shape by shape, as if it were a picture puzzle with funny-shaped parts. Keep checking the edges of the outline, measuring with your eyes, to make sure you are in the right place.

5. Don't turn your drawing around until you are done! When you do, you will be surprised.

ON YOUR OWN Now look around the room you are in. Can you look at a lamp, a chair, or even a jacket sleeve and see the simple shapes in them? Close one eye and trace the shapes in the air with your finger. That is the way an artist sees.

The One-Line Drawing

One of the things that makes a drawing beautiful is beautiful lines. Beautiful lines can be short and choppy, long and smooth, or wiggly. You decide on the type to match the picture. Following the instructions below, you will make a drawing with just a few long, smooth lines. The rules are: Each line must start from the edge of the border and end at a border. Your pencil can move in any direction in the drawing, and can even follow lines it has already drawn. However, **you cannot pick your pencil up from the paper,** except at the border.

1. For this drawing you will need a group of objects to copy that you have arranged in a corner on a table. This is called a still life. Try to find objects that are different shapes: tall and narrow, short and flat, squarish or roundish. They might be dinner table items such as a ketchup bottle, forks and knives, a cup and saucer, or a bowl. Arrange them close together so that their shapes overlap, but don't put any object directly in front of another. When you look at your arrangement from above, it could be like a diamond (see illustration **a.**). When you look at your arrangement from the side, it could be like a triangle, with taller items in back and shorter items in front.

a.

2. Draw a border on your paper. Your drawing must start at the edge of the border, so find an edge (like the edge of the table) your line can follow into the picture. Position yourself so that you can look up from your paper easily and see your tabletop arrangement. It might be helpful to attach your paper to a board, put the board on your lap, and lean it back against the edge of the tabletop.

3. Next draw the edge of the table. When you come to one of your objects, change direction to make its outline, then let your line flow into the next object. You don't need to finish each object as you go. You might draw the rim of a bowl with your first line, then finish the lower part of the bowl as you come back with your second line. Remember, as you draw each line, don't lift the pencil up from the paper. You can follow any edge. It might be the edge of a shadow on the table, a pattern on a label, or a highlight on something shiny. All of these have edges and are shapes.

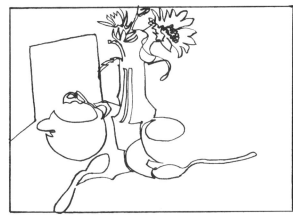

4. As you reach the top of the drawing, or the opposite edge, you can pick up the pencil. Start again somewhere else on the border, once more following an edge. Try to spend more time looking at the objects than you do looking at the whole drawing.

5. When you've drawn all the main edges, pick up your pencil. Notice that you don't just have a drawing of one object, but you have a whole scene, with a background as well. You have created a complete drawing with beautiful lines!

ON YOUR OWN   You can use this exercise to draw any subject. If you like to draw cars, horses, flowers, or jet planes, this will work. Get a model (even a photograph will do), draw a border, and start drawing from the edges inward.

Blind Drawing

If you have done the one-line drawing on pages 60–61, you are ready for blind drawing. You will need an object with some details for a model, like an interesting seashell, a toothbrush, a flower, or a bunch of keys. This is a drawing exercise to help you forget to say, "Oh, no, I drew it wrong!" and to stop you from erasing. It is a chance for you to forget about how the **drawing** looks and to concentrate on how the **model** looks. This will just be a drawing of a single object, not a complete picture with a frame.

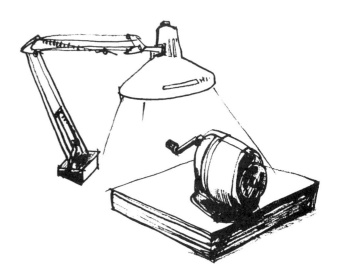

1. Attach your paper to a board and place the model on a table with good strong light on it. Get comfortable and decide what part of the model you will begin to draw. Place your pencil on the paper so there is plenty of room to draw the object without running off the page.

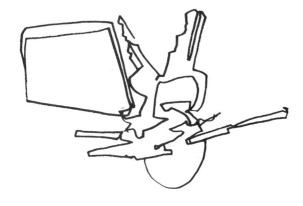

2. Now, **looking only at the model, not your paper,** and **keeping your pencil on the paper at all times,** draw the model.

3. As you did on pages 60–61, you may have to go over lines you have already made. Don't stop drawing, and don't look at your drawing until you are finished.

4. You should find yourself mentally crawling all over your model, your pencil following the curves and lines your eyes see, as if you were an ant. Your drawing should take at least ten minutes. When you have covered all the details, all the edges of the model, stop.

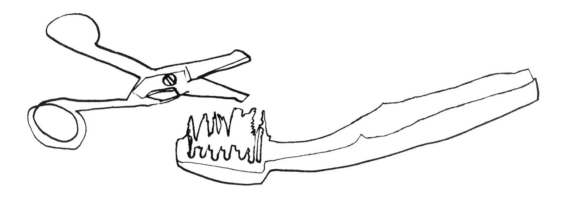

5. If you find that your drawing is out of proportion, or the lines don't meet, don't worry! What you will find, if you really tried to "blind draw," is a very beautiful line with lots of turning and twisting details you never had the patience to draw before. Blind drawing is not a way serious artists draw all the time.
It is an exercise they do to help them see the details in their models—and to concentrate on the models rather than the drawings.